ONE
SWEET
MOMENT

ESSENTIAL POETS SERIES 305

**Canada Council
for the Arts**

**Conseil des Arts
du Canada**

**ONTARIO ARTS COUNCIL
CONSEIL DES ARTS DE L'ONTARIO**

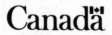

Guernica Editions Inc. acknowledges the support of the Canada Council
for the Arts and the Ontario Arts Council. The Ontario Arts Council
is an agency of the Government of Ontario.

We acknowledge the financial support of the Government of Canada.

BRUCE MEYER

ONE SWEET MOMENT

GUERNICA EDITIONS

TORONTO – CHICAGO – BUFFALO – LANCASTER (U.K.)

2023

Guernica Founder: Antonio D'Alfonso

Michael Mirolla, editor
Cover and Interior Design: Errol F. Richardson
Guernica Editions Inc.
287 Templemead Drive, Hamilton (ON), Canada L8W 2W4
2250 Military Road, Tonawanda, N.Y. 14150-6000 U.S.A.
www.guernicaeditions.com

Distributors:
Independent Publishers Group (IPG)
600 North Pulaski Road, Chicago IL 60624
University of Toronto Press Distribution (UTP)
5201 Dufferin Street, Toronto (ON), Canada M3H 5T8

First edition.
Printed in Canada.

Legal Deposit – Third Quarter
Library of Congress Catalog Card Number: 2022951917
Library and Archives Canada Cataloguing in Publication
Title: One sweet moment / Bruce Meyer.
Names: Meyer, Bruce, 1957- author.
Series: Essential poets ; 305.
Description: Series statement: Essential poets series ; 305 | Poems.
Identifiers: Canadiana 2023013324X | ISBN 9781771838290 (softcover)
Classification: LCC PS8576.E93 O54 2023 | DDC C811/.54—dc23

This world has only one sweet moment set aside for us

...

... Who dares to love forever

—**Queen**, "Who Wants to Live Forever"

for Kerry, Katie, Margaret, and Carolyn

Contents

Friendship is a Summer that Never Sheds Its Leaves

My grandfather's boyhood friend
would visit on a long June afternoon,

and when it came time for him to leave,
I would walk the old men to the corner bus

that ran south toward the city. Everything
is gone now, the friends, sparking trolley

cables, though destinations remain the same,
as ingrained in the city's face as streets,

arteries of lots and square-built houses,
the one-way pavement of roads laid out

in the waffle iron grid of a surveyor's sight,
the pattern of stories passed from one

narrator to another. I retain images from
those afternoons because I cannot forget

the heat outside the pharmacy's door,
the tiles in which someone had set a green

message of prescription signed Rx,
remaining where the drugstore stood.

The shelves and displays smelt of cloves
to lay upon an aching tooth, and mint

to cover the aftertaste that growing old
can bring, green as the pattern of tiles

that could have doubled as a chessboard
where knights awaited their next move.

Mount Everest

George Mallory's grasp gave way
and he lay on the slope for ninety years.
His hands were still as pale as maps,
and in his pocket were his love notes,
comparing the courage of a climb
to the breathlessness of a heart in passion.

Reaching for heights is a fool's sport.
When I see poetry books set out at the curb,
their covers grimacing as if frozen alive,
I wonder why anyone would write them.
Their inspiration thins with time,
until each breathless word fades out;

yet someone had the courage to write them
because it is there and needed to be said.
Their titles are excuses for audacity;
and when I remember a single line,
I think of the view from Everest's peak,
the world's incisor smiling at the sky,
having bitten off a taste of heaven
and asking that it be described in words
to someone in an English garden
where rosebuds gather praise from bees.

Teaching Dante to Priests

Hotter than Hell in the classroom,
the two-hour lecture with readings
began with a discussion of language
and how Dante uses the Cardinal
or narrative form of expression
to make the Inferno into Storytime.

Who doesn't love a lengthy explanation
when there's an eternity to kill,
full of cause and effect with some remorse
that made the class of ten urban priests
respond to the humid summer morning
by removing their soot-colored coats?

They resembled beaded, greasy seagulls.
In Purgatory it was obvious they had
asked their bishops for favors of grace.
Next to go were clergy shirts and collars,
until they resembled a plot of gardeners
as their shirts clung to their guts and chests.

This world, written in the vulgar tongue,
speaks volumes of who we really are,
the truth made flesh and the flesh hairy
when the mask of vestments is removed
and the secret of their humanity is revealed.
Ordained, they work their miracles.

Had it not been for their tank-top underwear
they could have been confused for bankers
out for an impromptu picnic or salesmen
weary from carrying their load of goods
and yet there was something illustrious
about their melodious rhetoric as they asked

questions about the brevity of every virtue
carried on the updraft of empyrean grace.
That is when my boss walked in, startled
to see her shepherds in their underwear,
and said she didn't want to know why.
Accepting mysteries is part of reading Dante

and perhaps that is the gift of the poet
who not only showed the world the blindness
that comes from looking upon true light
in all its naked humility, but the blessing
of human unity. We are all equal in sin
and forgiveness saith the Almighty.

After all, the stars are made of fire,
invisible by day but shining nonetheless,
burning with the holy spirit that passes
through the naked arms of summer maples
rattling their leaves outside my classroom
where my charges gathered for their synod

during the break to discuss the finer points
of being alone in the world with nothing
but the gift of words and the salt bread
of strangers for succor and sustenance,
the charity of a distant god who makes
pilgrims lose their sight so they can see.

Where My Father Went

Autumn mornings I would wake
and find my father had returned
in the night from faraway places
I could barely imagine, his cheeks

stubbled and greasy from factories
where working men stood long hours
at their lathes, souls on the threshold
of a scream, and their jokes raw.

I would try to picture those distant
towns spread across America
like stars fallen from a broken dream
and couldn't picture what their names

described: Raw Bend and Tall Corn,
and pictured him peering through stalks
in mazes of thick green crops,
each fallen ear listening to the world.

His secret life was so far beyond me
I felt the strange gift of his return
on silent wings and moonlit winds
in the mornings of my waking,

and tears carried on the currents
of disbelief so unfathomably bleak
they ached to answer the void he left
that would take a lifetime to fill.

I shall have to retrace my path
to the days we were together
and meet him midway, staggered
at all the goodbyes we never said

or where we'd been when we returned,
never saying hello yet assuming
we'd be there the next time like a door
that opened with a key to my heart.

Shift

In the checkout line at the grocery store,
as the cashier rings in last fall's apples,

I glance out the plate glass window at the sunset
and I ask if she understands how the universe changes

and how little things make a night of difference.
Her feet are aching from standing in one spot

the way a tree puts down roots yet lives for the moment.
She wants to finish her shift and go home,

and that's all there is to it – just finish the day
and leave the dreaming to shoppers

so she doesn't have to do more work,
so at the end of her shift that began this morning

she can shake the stars from her leafless hair
and quietly slip into the trance of autumn.

Snow Geese

Looking down on the world
as it woke from winter,
I saw the hills and fields
shedding the last vestiges

of paralysis; the big river
below, the plane running east,
the small towns spread
like a child's drawings

on the floor, and the edges
of cities we flew over casting
wing shadows on the streets
when I spotted the snow geese.

At first, I thought they were
clouds a factory had spewed,
but the farther north the flocks
flew, the more intricately

I saw the fine angles
of their black-tipped wings,
their oars of white feathers
rowing the air hard

with a sense of determination
in every stroke. You leaned
over and said they were
beautiful, but as you sat back

they were more than mere
objects to admire below;
they were part of a world
that stood still too long,

part of the currents freed in
frozen rivers, the sap
coursing in the trees at last,
the sun finally meaning light,

and their goosenecks straining
against a flight path north,
and the unison of motion
with their leader that amazed me

to the point I wanted to say
a prayer though I don't
pray much except to utter
words that seem so small

in comparison to the horizon,
the Earth's surface curving
as if the day had bent it
around the cloudless sky;

and I was filled with joy
at seeing the unexpected
because what surprises us is
not the world but the way

it overcomes, the way a poem
appears out of thin air,
not because some things belong
in words but because they can't

be held still by them, a drive
the body can't contain
in a posture of toughness
or sneers at poems of joy

because there are times
when a moment leaps up and flies,
and the mind shouts back
it deserves this wonder,

as snow geese stroke the air
harder to demonstrate
how miracles can be real
and there's blood in every vein.

Tadpoles

At first, they were commas
punctuating the muddy depths,

before morphing into hurried dashes
and stilling to periods among the reeds.

My grandfather said ancient pens
were made from reed snippets by the shore,

and to prove his point with an edge
opened his pocket knife to trim a stem,,

then dipped the point in the brown pond
and wrote the word *tadpole* on a sunburnt stone,

and watched the words pale or leap
onto a page of vanishing sunlit ink.

The Last Dodo in Madagascar Gave Us the Beauty of Fear

Think of madness as a baobab
forest where the sloths cling
to the highest branches to feel
the world moving slowly below
them as a piece of fruit ripened
beyond the limits of sweetness

they stare at the frightened floor
amid decaying leaves scattered
like maxims for a philosopher
and are glad at working to learn
the lessons of necessity fall back
on fears. So many places lie in

ruins. No one thinks of paradise
or what hid behind its iron gate.
Yet the sloths understand what
kept the dodos alive for so long,
the power of the mind is joy
knowing joy remained in Eden.

Time began in earnest with that idea.
Time changes everything, gave us
the dodo, that apex of heroic charm,
in such a charming and determined way
the birds never thought they'd die.
Fearlessness is the courageous failure

to forget why fears exist, the loneliness
of distant stars poking at a wonder
that repeats its name like daybreak.
Dodos never learned to fear,
even if embracing such fearlessness
meant the bird brought on its own demise.

What lacks a shred of forethought in its
heart loves this world too much to foresee
its death. A bald vulture spreads its
wings across the night and prepares
to eat the remnants of a kill. The cries
of a bleeding infant sloth or meat

that grew wise enough to marvel
at the beauty of life and hold onto it
was real, the echo of a flightless smile
on two squat legs, begging an exception
to what one is supposed to believe,
and why everything desires to be loved

and not merely loved by its own kind
but by the force of fear, is the realization
each life must end but has no idea why.
Fear protects life, and the dodo betrayed
us all, incapable of foreseeing a broken
world when it approached us with

its hook-beaked lips and mouth large
enough to hold Eden in its simple awe.
The past was almost like the present
with one exception: we fear more now.
It gave us the avuncular gift of kindness
to fight for the world and stay alive.

Taking Stock

Between the idling cars trapped
at the four-way intersection,
the veal calf ran for its life,
stopping to splay on the hood

of the family car, legs kicking
ferociously to fight the world.
Everything wants to be free.
Instinct is the refusal to give up.

That's why my father refused
to go near Jane and St. Clair:
the corner carried a memory
from a childhood nightmare,

until one day we were stuck
in traffic, he admitted, his voice
breaking, to fearing a glaze
in a calf's eyes, a look far more

terrible than the stench of sudden
death. the police were closing
the ring, guns unholstered, the captain
shouting "Don't shoot!"

My Dad prayed for a miracle,
but only horses fly and they
are barely broken, leaping
clear of their pale pathetic horror,

driven between cars and snared.
An hour or two later, bravery did
the calf no good. It was blinded by
a darkness impossible to comprehend.

There was nothing the young bovine
could do. Helplessness is a malady
all creatures have in common watching
behind windshields or dark eyes.

The Work

Saturday afternoons when I accompanied my father
on his weekend errands, he would dial the dashboard

radio to broadcasts from the Metropolitan Opera
where a man with a mid-Atlantic accent explained

the grief of human calamity set to song. When traffic
snarled and a soprano lamented how she gave her

life to art while her lover was tortured just off stage,
my father would stare at the long avenues ahead,

and one day he told me he'd taken singing lessons
but the road did not go where he had hoped and fate

always plays a hand in what we are, though we sing
when no one listens to how it could be different.

Bleeding Heart

In my mother's garden, her favorite flower
was a root her uncle dug for her
from his farm near Lake Erie's shore.
It was something with meaning for her aunt,
a relic of a time when flowers were feelings
and a single bloom spoke of sadness.

Each small pink heart opened to a tear,
a sacred promise someone broke,
a month of happiness over far too soon,
and remembered in a flower.

She would snip a sprig and arrange it with roses
nestled among lily of the valley bells
because those were the first blooms of summer,
and adorned her mother's bridal veil
when she gave herself to the promise of life,
knowing what grows best to its heart's content
is rooted in shade with full morning sun.

The Twilight

The street hockey boys
make twilight last for hours
until the air freezes their pantlegs.

Beneath grapefruit streetlamps
their sour, milky breaths,
sweet at first as cotton candy,

are driven to shouts of triumph
by an insatiable desire
for fame and warm beds

and small, curtained rooms,
and like sleeping cats
huddled in frigid alleyways

carved in snowdrifts between the houses,
warm their fingers on a flame
that should, by rights, be eternal

but in truth is barely the flickering
of a match struck in a north wind,
the magic that consumes its brilliance.

Like

Yes. I like you. I really
like you like an actress
at the Oscars overcome

by a moment like no other
and feeling that instant
of bliss that made everyone

like her even more for making
them happy too, and like
the wonder of liking what

one wishes to like and not
apologizing for the pleasure
that liking brings –

the compassion of learning
how to like the unknown
like something that reminds

us of what we already know
and discover it is like
a definition of discovery

not just two hearts
likened to stems on a rose
intertwined around each

other like shadows meeting
on a wall and embracing
and becoming one.

You show me things just
as if you shone a flashlight
on a problem and I could

see the details of it and
there is more to it than I
ever imagined like blades

of grass seemingly green
but each unique on its own
like a flower or a tree

and maybe all that remains
for us to do like a final
herculean task is to like

giving and receiving
absolution and kindness
from each other and like

so many others I like you
for doing that and maybe
more because I, too,

do not simply like you
but feel a force deeper
than similitude can like,

or to put it another way,
I not only like you.
I more than like you.

Gorse on a June Day: Elegy for Seamus Heaney

Returning to Dublin on a rare
overheated June afternoon
when we stood with a hard day

in our hair and listened silently
to the crackling of the gorse
and watched as the hedgerows

burst from yellow into green,
we drove along Strand Road
as the poet tried to cure

the rhythm of his car's meter.
Everything possesses the need
to follow patterns: a clock

as the day wound down,
the engine that rhymed pulses
with all its soul in the bonnet.

He saw his work was good
and wiping his hands on a rag
he bent over the working parts

and listened intently. A poem
emerged from the fan belt,
a song driven by pistons sang

with the beauty of the world,
and he shut it, and stepped away
as creators do to admire it all.

The last time we spoke, he
told me we'd have a pint
someday in Dublin, but by

the time I finally had the time
he suffered from a poor heart
and my illness says I cannot

toast him now. So, here is
my imaginary pint, the spirit
of the glass that opens gorse,

and the hand that moves over
lush valleys greener than
any poem could describe.

Time and I finally arrived
in the same place and found
everything had changed,

like the tide that pressed
the sea for its return, the
wind that fell like words

from silver clouds and spit
at them the way an old
man's speech is full of rain

like the wind on the west coast.
The weather in Sligo was
raw and Irish, yet I marveled

at the defiance of the human
state, the blood as warm in me
as the air exhaled by an oven

while a woman baked her
loaves and flew a goose's
wing free of its extra meal

before returning it to her
bin. She has been about
her work since dawn

and the aroma of fresh
loaves fills the house with
the fragrances of necessity

and love. She opens
the oven door and grasps
between folds of cloth

the hot pan and the joy
it holds that is poetry
to the hungry mouth.

Pulling up a chair beside
her table, she takes a load
off her measling shins,

and thinks the kitchen
as warm as a miraculous
day when life opened to let

sunlight touch the small
glints that pass through, not just
to be born from the green

that spreads its life upon
the island but are transfigured
by the works of wonders.

That, he acknowledged,
is what poetry does,
the bursting of blossoms,

the land changed by magic.
Such is the power of words.
The air sings with green.

Dancing in Shona's Rec Room

Had it not been for the knotty-eyed paneling,
the grey, and white linoleum tiled floor,

and the half-window curtains that hung
like bath towels from startled older sisters,

we might have been in heaven. Bread
spun on the hi-fi. The lights were low.

The room had an aura of a seediness
we craved in our dreams though dreams

never ended badly except when we awoke.
Martha Hunter pressed me close. I could feel

her freckled breath upon my neck; could know
the warmth of her body next to mine;

the brush of her thighs against my thighs;
the embrace that left no space between us

except the tottering of a failed dance.
There was a time when sex wasn't sex.

Years later as I kiss my wife goodnight,
her hair and body dripping as she steps

from the shower after a long day's work,
I feel a tuberous attachment to her

the way potatoes in a field love being grounded
no matter how cold the earth around them.

But Shona's rec room was the reality
I thought life could become, the dreamland

where love songs were three minutes of hope;
and as I pressed Martha closer she recoiled.

I could not help myself, I'd tell her now.
I was a boy in love with boyish dreams,

a body so beyond my knowledge I feared it
the way one fears the future.

She died of cancer twenty years ago
leaving two grown children and a husband

who must have danced with her and spoken
to her being the way lightning speaks to trees.

Apiary

The lavender fields are dotted
with white boxes squat as houses.

In his mesh veil, smoker handy,
hands gloved, he slowly removes

the upright tray patterned in perfect
hexagons of wax, lifting it gently

with a swarm on it as if a painting
come to life to speak of life.

He calls it the sweetness of being.
He explains why the hive spends

every moment of living daylight
to capture the deep scent of purple.

Honey has the taste of wisdom,
the reason I have come at sunset

with a need to know the work of bees,
hoping that just one word of truth

with be enough to satisfy my lips.
He tells me the best honey is love,

born from pleasure and hard work,
spooned upon my fingertip

as we stand at his kitchen table
and sample the labor of a day.

The sun is pressing on the horizon
and reminds me of my promises,

and the amber afterglow of words
I want to carry home and live by

because every waking moment
is spun clean from its beginning

and waits to be released from wax,
a promise freed from sincerity

when it is kept. This is not wisdom
but the love of knowing its sting.

Desiring Milkweed

I ask my student to picture herself
on a late summer afternoon, alone

in the stillness of a rural road
with a hill rising before her and ditches

lined with milkweed pods bursting
to release an enormous gasp of seeds.

My student asks what she should
write about – the milk or the weed

for she has been taught to see the world
in a binary system of either/or.

I tell her I don't know. The choice
is hers alone. She worries she is

wrong. In a poem, there are no
absolutes, just choices. I ask if

milkweed can be both milk and weed
(compound noun, notwithstanding)

and having said that I won't tell her
there are phoebes perched on wires

overhead along the dusty gravel road
and sometimes the birds descend to sit

for hours swaying in the breeze atop
bullrushes in a ditch on the ripe pods

of milkweed, balancing on their shadows.
There is no right or wrong thing

to write about the truth of the world
or words to describe their chirping song

when only singing matters – the birds'
or hers – or if the bird cares what it makes

or what it desires beyond all words.

Epiphanies

Beyond the point
of any perception –
staring at a field
and blind by snow,

the crow's outline,
like a comma
on an empty page,
waits for syntax

to punctuate the truth
and work its magic –
and far from death
or too close

to peck a mouse,
is a moot point;
and even the crow
lives in fear

and awe that snow
and sunlight blind
us both so we must
imagine our own miracles.

Symbols

Our daughter framed a mandala
and hung it over her computer desk
to describe how heaven spoke to Earth
on days when no one wanted to speak.
In the dining room, a candelabra
with seven branches was a dream
of a man whose familial ambitions
lit a shining stairway to heaven
unlike the celadon garage sale Confucius
that stood halfway up the stairs,
its silence an analect against striving
to reach the second floor by want.
He guarded pussy-willows in a butterfly vase.
In the family room, twenty-seven suns
hung on the long wall above the shelves
where hot jazz recordings sat, some
with the salsa of an Aztec sunrise
while others, more mysterious, sang
in the starry reticence of an African night.
Over the entrance, we nailed a Celtic cross
with a ring at the intersection point
of time and eternity to remind us
that beyond the finite and the infinite
waits a spirit to call its home, welcomes
travellers whose roads rose with them
because being here and being alive
is a matter of climbing the tree of life
that sprouted on a boho throw we cast
to a mask a fraying second-hand chair
where a guest could sit and feel divine.

Monarch

Few people drive along Highway 6
but you always conspired to slow and look
when we reached the crest
with the hayfields before us
and shimmering asphalt in the late day light.

One afternoon you opened the door
and without looking to see if anyone approached,
stooped for a monarch to find your index,
its small black legs climbing your finger
as if it knew you were a kindness tree.

You eased it into a roadside thicket
where a dozen milkweed flowers bloomed
and it held on tight as it swayed in the wind –

and if more than dust is born on the wind
so just one breath inspires the plants and insects,
I whisper how you inspire me
as I wait breathlessly for your reply.

You draw in the day and exhale the sun.

Indigo

Duke Ellington composed *Mood Indigo*
while waiting for his mother
to cook dinner. Home cooking

has its own melody. All he had
to do was listen. I ask myself
what aroma would inspire

the clear dawn sky on a morning
so cold January surrendered,
and how the darkness knelt

before the purple robes of dawn
as sunlight crowned the new day.
In the distance, a plume of steam

rose from a house across the lake,
and its windows opened their eyes
not because the place personified

anything other than a dwelling,
but because beneath warm blankets,
someone needed to know how kings

bow to heaven. A dog howled
as dinner was served. Tasted first,
he devoured each helping with passion.

Bakelite

Her man ran off with a woman who promised
to buy him a new tractor. A preacher said the work
of God was mysterious as wind racing to bless

the head of every stalk of corn. The Sioux City
Bears were leading by six going into the ninth.
Perry Como wanted a little dreamer to dream on.

The radio in my headboard was a prophet eating
locusts in the Midwest dust, and a prairie fire
in the buzzing clock insisted now was three a.m.,

that if I closed my eyes there wasn't any far away,
no highway straight as a salesman's spiel,
or limits to the miles my ear could see.

The Beautiful Neanderthals

They never knew that they were different
from sunlight at the open mouth
of a smoky cave or the fragile flames of flowers
they gave the dead to remind themselves .
that summer grows from winter days
when even the sky is tired of life.

They never saw any difference
between the sand they walked on and their footprints
or the waves that carried their marks away,
or the trees that tried to catch the wind
and spoke of it as being hurried
when it would not stay to share its stories.

They loved each other as they loved the stars
when they lay on beaches of ancient seas
and took comfort from their own forevers
that fed them legends of small tomorrows
where game was plentiful and every eye
measured the dance of shadows as life.

They knew how to solve eternal questions,
but never asked them for fear the answers
might be different if the moon was full.
The seas rose. Their forests vanished.
They owned an afterlife as they owned their lives,
and what was left they grew to love,

for none knew they were any different
from the long chins who came to love them,
passing from gene to gene their tiny secrets
of a world so hard to love it failed –
and still, they loved it. Winter came. The oceans froze.
They wept for all the starry blossoms,

for the frozen bodies of the birds they knew,
for the ibexes and swift-hind gazelles
that made life worth the pain of beauty,
never knowing that each living thing
was something different from their beating hearts:
they loved greatly the greatness in all love,

and vanished quietly in the silence of flowers
opening their blossoms like hearts to truths
to find the secrets that embrace all things,
the whisper of wind that speaks one name,
the waves of oceans that are one sea,
the mountains in every grain of sand.

Meteor

We were driving home in twilight
at the end of a long spring day.
The baby slept in her car seat.
A murmuration of starlings
shifted shape above a barn

as a gash of light cut the afterglow.
At first, I thought a blade of sky
had broken off the day

and houses with their lights on
at the end of rutted lanes
were usual as the unusual can be

when I looked with astonishment
at the darkness of the highway ahead
and realized how little I know.

Rising Water

Four years ago I traced this shore.
My footprints threaded needles of reeds.
Thin grasses. Dry, flat rocks.
Waves of limestone lapped by wind
when afternoon sunlight made skillets of slabs.

Four years ago I could walk this shore.
Pick up fossils of coral reef shards.
Could turn over rocks between my fingers.
The world loves water
until there's too much of it.

The water this year reached a record high,
refuting all my ideas of shore
between the cobbled wash
and leaning cedars
that spent their lives trying not to fall down.

These words are all that remain of the shore.
Next year, or perhaps a year after,
nothing will say a shoreline ran here,
except a line I want to imagine,
the thread of words submerged in a poem.

On First Looking into Bark's Rumi

Without ever desiring to cast a dying shadow
to show a wanderer where he has travelled,
I have thought of souls and mortgaged souls,

and how, in the solitary cold of distant time,
the stars I wished on died before their light
became worthy of a moment's poetry;

how by the incessant presence of my life
I have tried to grasp the purpose of living
and comprehend the intentions of the world,

and struggled to know how to answer.
I have waited in the twisted moonlight
and stood with others in the wrath of sun,

to hear an answer beyond good or evil
whose actors were poorly scripted as they played
in my strange and savage comedy.

And there have been times when being alone
has been as pleasant as a morning walk
along a beach as the tide rolled out and broken

things revealed themselves to me as lovers
waiting for an explanation or a passing word
about a bowl of rosewater or a murdered rose,

and the complexity of words to offer friendship,
when knowing another reaches its sad end
and only the silence of the soul knows better,

or knows love, or knows nothing, and the stars
have something lasting to say about a place
where there is little to say and only silence hears it.

Renoir and the Bather in the Woods

Removing my glasses, this is what I saw:
the blurred, myopic vision, the flow
of colour into colour and the light
touching her shoulders and thighs said
the moment was neither right nor wrong,
and nothing lives outside its frame.

I close my eyes for a moment. I frame
a picture in my mind of what I saw –
light in late afternoon, the wrong
reflection of sienna and white, a flow
of oil on palette – these things said
life was a work in progress, the light

that touched what the eye imagines, a light
hiding like heaven in the mind, the frame
of limitations and what cannot be said
or sketched, the failed beauty I saw
for a moment in a brush stroke, the flow
of ink tasting canvas, and the wrong

medium for stroking flesh. Am I wrong
to close my eyes and watch the light
twist into a vision of beauty, the flow
of breath becoming a woman in a frame,
and the frame holding it all in? I saw
a world hold its breath as everything said,

"You can do better." I should have said
that colour only describes what is wrong
with what one sees; colours stutter and flow
one into the other, the way late daylight
is a *trompe l'oeil* the eye must frame
for an instant and then forget, the flow

of image no memory can contain, the flow
of a stream where she stands; and when all is said
and done, life *cannot* be held in a frame.
Vision is an illusion. Sight is an idea wrong
before it can be made right, the light
of the moment she looked at me and I saw

an angelic host flow from the wrong end of time
in search of a beginning. Who said the light
in a frame lasts forever? I saw her vanish.

Reception

The snow is falling harder than the silence
and through the front window of the office
he sees the flakes running from the night
and falling in desperation on the glass.

For such a foul night, no one has come in
to rent a room. He imagines the door opening,
a passion of flakes blowing in behind a traveller
who is tired of fighting the highway, the roads

are empty as the heart, the highway closed
by the police, and good intentions paved
in frozen sky. He wonders if there's a heaven,
if prayers are heard and blessings delivered.

Good intentions are hard to come by on a night
like this. Lonely motorists on the interstate
must be dreaming of a tired motel like this.
He stares over the mountain of the front desk

as the ice machine in the lobby rattles to life
and he finds the irony cold and delightful
and the moment a punctuation of his life –
the beauty that doesn't need a gift placed

before him. Yes. Perhaps there is a heaven
where each snowflake is forged on the anvil
of the Lord. Proving its existence is impossible
like looking for blades of grass beneath the snow.

The August Rain

His last day with the window open,
I had to break the news to him:
he would not be able to die at home.

He trusted me and I broke his heart,
telling him what no one else dared say
as the last light of a humid August

threaded the shadows of fattened leaves
that counted down their days to fall.
In the ambulance when I reached out

to hold his hand he snatched it back,
then turned his face away from me
with a silence that spoke only of betrayal.

The streets he'd known all his life
were reeled in like a measuring tape,
but the last thing he said as he left his room,

was to tell the attendants to close the sash
in case it rained and leaves blew in.

Keeping Time as a Pet

Nosing into the future, white around the muzzle,
it sleeps half the day in sunlight
spread on the living room floor.

We love the year because it has been with us
for so long, because it has grown familiar
and has become our own.

Keeping time as a pet is a matter of belonging,
of saying we cannot live without its
snoring and panting. Such things bring comfort.

It surprises us when it chases its desires,
strains at the tether of patience
to satisfy its sudden urges,

and the longer it remains with us
the more we love it, faithful, obedient,
it is our year. It is a good year.

Jasmine Tea

When water touched their sleeping buds
the jasmine flowers opened as *pinyin*
then floated to the surface
the way thoughts become a poem
and blossom into words.

My father would put his ear to the lip
and listen to what the blossoms said
as they renewed their lives in warm spring rain.

He would offer me a sip of April,
though April was never as perfumed
as the music I am certain he heard
when he closed his eyes, inhaled the fragrance
rising in tendrils of curling steam
steeped in legend and a rice-grained bowl.

The Best Time to Grow a Beard

I argue the best time to grow a beard
is when travelling and no one says
You're looking rather rough these days.

Everyone is out of place somewhere,
yet the element of old presumptions
is missing from the eyes of strangers.

They will pass you in a street at dawn,
having never laid eyes on you before
or remember when your face was *clean*.

They will behold you as you behold
tomorrow while dawdling the night before
when stars took shelter in darkened doorways

and you mastered your personal geography,
the foreign feel of hand on chin,
the sudden itch when you tried to smile

when you pictured rounding another corner
and its intersection of possibilities,
a crosswalk like a flattened zebra,

a post box for letters you haven't penned,
a quiet you won't break by singing,
a parked car with its flashers blinking,

as if awakened from a long deep sleep
where you passed shop windows and didn't know
the face looking back at you was yours

because the snowy layer upon your chin
suggests you have come by wisdom,
though there's not a whisker of truth to it;

and if need be, you can act the beggar,
with a beard half there and a faraway look,
suggesting you have much farther to go.

Poets of the Late Shang Dynasty

The poets saw the mountains first
from far away, saw the slopes

as beggars sleeping at the strewn crest
where the summit sloped away

to foothills awakened at first light
and grew from long blue dreams

where a tree bough over-hung the way
after a dawn rain washed it clean,

thirsting for words to comfort them
through dry months of rocky summers

when a harvest of high dust clouds
promised another year of hardship.

The poets saw a rich, green harvest
and compared it to a faithful servant.

Mountains became dragon teeth,
yawning at heaven with hungry prayers,

knowing that poetry must invent
a language to describe the long way back,

reminding others to leave messages too
if they wanted to follow the difficult road,

where the mountain offers equal hardship –
the shade beside a quick brook across the path

not just to slake a traveler's thirst
but to sparkle as it touched the sun.

The last of the early Shang poets
was asked if mountains are made of words.

He shook his head and poured a ladle
of sunlight so clear it could have been water.

Starting School

She was proud of her sky-blue slicker
and the bright yellow rainboots

that reminded her of duck's feet.
When I left her at the school door,

she turned to wave goodbye to me.
Rain was dancing on my umbrella,

falling in a veil like a curtain drawn
across her future or an eye blinking

in surprise. I went off to work,
desiring to learn the world by heart.

Streets

The street where I put down roots –
the street where I kissed you once,

the street where I would find
an all-night coffee shop open

after the pubs had closed, the shop
that sold only doughnut holes,

the street where I bought a present
to surprise you and I counted starlings

and admonished them for bleating
their secrets, and the quarters I fed a space

so the meter maid would not break
the perfect spell of poetry that night,

the street where I saw my reflection
in a window and realized I was not

the youth you fell in love with
but someone who doubted himself

and knew there wouldn't be enough life
for all the answers or even the questions –

we walked together for a block or two
before you turned to meet someone

or told me something I didn't know,
or shared a ripe apple you carried,

and how we both inhabited the street
where wind tousled our hair until we laughed

and could not find an address we knew ...
the street that disappears in the distance,

and we know, if we follow it all the way
time will make us disappear as well.

The Apple Peeler

When it fell from a wooden box
stored on a cellar shelf, she explained
how it worked, and never worked
the way it was intended, its blade

biting too deep into the fruit's soft flesh,
and turning the orb to a baluster;
yet having been consigned
to history, the handle still cranked

and the gears responded, spinning
pronged spikes like compass needles.
The blade had gone rusty and if used
left a trail of blood around the girth

of all it mapped on an apple globe,
the awful history that brought us here.

Home Run

After the sun goes down and I am alone,
I stretch on the cool grass, run my fingers

over it, and wonder if success isn't another lie
people tell themselves to excuse perfection

when what becomes tomorrow is hard work
and they need to make it happen all over again.

Portrait of My Mother as a Bone China Figurine

You let me hold your Doulton figurine
one afternoon when I was three
and your yellow hair and long pink dress,
your entire frame from head to toe,
was the size of my outstretched hand.

Use both hands. Handle with care.
You told me the woman who gave it to you
thought it resembled you as a child,
a figure about to kneel in curtsy,
poised on a translucent magic
with a pumpkin carriage waiting
outside your door.

I have not dared to hold her since,
never wanted to cradle her in my hands
and ask her for a dance
(though one afternoon you tried to teach me
how to waltz knowing it was the lost art
of stepping lightly and holding gently

and everything I touched grew weightless
as a falling leaf caught in the spiral of time).
Light passes through your hands now
the way it passes through fine bone china,
a translucence describing how to touch things
with the soft feel of care;

and even in my mind as I see her dress,
floor-length, pink, with a low-cut neckline,
I extended my hand to the first girl I danced with
and she acknowledged it with grace.

View-Master

In the drafty spare front room
    when he lay down for a nap,
I would sit beside him,
    aware he couldn't hear me,

and click through View-Master discs —
    palaces of toppled monarchs,
canyons deeper than griefs,
    and streets where capitols

rose above the traffic noises
    with domes of glistening marble
ice white in the morning light.
    The weather was always perfect,

the image a reminder of marvels
    I longed to see for myself,
my forbidden travels into life.
    All I knew was monochrome,

crowded into a tiny space
    where days were photographs
closed in the covers of a book.
    When he woke I asked him

if dreams had three dimensions,
    if tucking praying hands
beneath his good ear as he slept
    helped him catch the songs of angels

as his thoughts shot up to heaven.
    Could I have dreams like that?
He closed his eyes to remember
    but he lost his thoughts along the way.

War Work

For two weeks they work on a new design
for a gun-mount motor, measuring each part,
reading tables of blueprints, checking the specs,
and discussing solutions to problems they faced
when they weren't past their elbows in PCBs,
or loosening bolts and removing housings,
or shaving and filing the parts, the ends of threads
to make metal fit against metal
so a powerful current could run through the coils
and make the machine leap to life.

Suddenly, one among them snaps to attention,
his eyes wide, drawn back in their sockets,
and before anyone can shut off the power
the startled man is dead where he stands.
They kill the current and he falls to the floor.

The other workmen gather around.
One of them runs to fetch a medic,
but those nearest know the smell of boiled flesh,
the singe on the dead man's lips and fingers,
and the look of amazement on his face.

A stretcher arrives with three factory nurses,
one to cover the dead man's body,
unfolding the linen from its clean pressed square,
and two for the stretcher to bear the body.
No one realizes the motor is still in his hands
as volts ran through his spasmed limbs
or saw him going stiff as a board.

The workers on the floor return to their tasks
and the noise of the lathes means each is alone
to say what they want without being heard.
There are deadlines they have to meet.
Everyone has a war to win.

In the infirmary, the dead man's friend
tells him the test went well this time,
that whatever passed between him and his life
made the motor whirr and spin.

He pulls back the sheet on the dead man's face.
and marvels at the look of joy on his face,
astonished at how an invisible power,
a force bringing light to a windowless room,
has stopped his friend's heart while holding him stiff,
and he thinks of telling him a joke from the floor,
how some men play with sparks until they leap free.
She must have been good to make him smile that way.

But instead, he eases the sheet back in place,
tells him to get a good night's sleep,
and imagine the hum of the motor they built
and the sound he hears in the depth of night,
are the heavy breaths are the girl beside him.

Sea Turtles

Memory is a savage place,
where going to meet defeat

seems the right thing to do,
before being picked-off

by a seabird or waiting shark;
this defines a sea turtle,

thinking only of a destination
as the green surf rushes in; ask

the turtle where it will go or if
it knows this beach is home

and must return someday.
Currents pull on undersea wings.

How can life be forgiven for
what it offers then takes away?

Songbird

Memory only stretches so far
before it loses the shape it once had:

Two women talk on the sidewalk,
one with her arms crossed; is the other

pointing at a problem with her roof?
A child falls off his bicycle

and an empty bus brakes at the light.
In case the past is going out of fashion

ask the songbird who didn't have
the strength to leave as autumn came,

the milkweed seed that never flew
because memory held on to all its wishes.

He still sings to wake me at dawn
especially on days as warm as today

when the sun tries to recall the summer
though the bird's song goes unanswered

and he can't remember why …

The Crease

With the wind in their faces,
they chased their breath
as it chased the stars above,

their effort exhausting
the illusion of small glory.
They wanted to be heroes.

Growing up meant heeding
the call of parents to come
home from the local rink

to waiting books of homework
and chill blain baths
and the promise that tomorrow,

if the cold snap held another
day or two the ice would be
swift and solid and someone,

perhaps a father, would stand
on the silver sheet, hose in hand
and pave the park in tomorrows.

One boy stick-handled three miles
on the surface of Lake Superior
only to find the absence of a net.

Each night they would pray
to the faith of becoming
the impossible hope in which

boys live and adults die in,
the goal always waiting
yet so far, so very, very far.

Windowpane Story

Frost is the cursive script of a long story,
describing who will be touched by love –

and who will be getting dressed for work,
and lie down, too tired to leave.

Tell me frost who you need to know next.
Even the worst winters are certain to end.

I take my fingernail and scrape a peephole.
The trees, shrubs, grass, and leaves

are weighted with white as if you are alive
and everything you breathe is someone else's breath.

I have seen your pattern on galvanized steel.
What you cling to was struck by lightning.

Boyhood

There were valleys where
streams chased their lost
passions and willows

admired what might become
of us someday when the beach
could not hold back the tide.

It was a time of outgrowing
the dominion of small things,
though holding them

in the palm of my hand
brought wonder to my eyes
until everything grew too small to see.

The Minerva Knocker

The head of the goddess Minerva
protruded from the front door
of the old house where you lived
in a second-floor apartment.

Heroes found her irresistible,
and nineteenth-century foundries
cast her as a voice of welcome
and farewell, so visitors knocked

upon arrival and those departing
would hear the sound of her harp
bouncing on the hob behind them.
She was patron of the creative arts,

and therein lies the truth of her:
the new arrives in the world
and the old resonates in departure,
and that is why I loved to kiss you

on your front porch with the door
open, sometimes coming, sometimes going,
as if we were a page in a notebook
and our lives the pen to write the story.

Watching the Perseid Meteor Shower on the Beach at Point Pelee

To see a falling star and say one's name
before the thread of light burns out

is to be granted an impossible wish:
gamblers, we thought the next good star

would be our pay-off; sand in our shoes,
made our way through a narrow dune,

among invisible bodies on the beach,
through breaths synchronized to the hush

of waves smoothed sober on the shore.
We ventured the lights far to the south

were Toledo, perhaps Sandusky, the glow
to the north possibly Windsor or Detroit,

and the line between the lake and sky
as indistinct as those strewn beside us,

and it staggered our imaginations.
Falling stars are too brief for words.

Having made their way through time,
traversed the vacuum of space and silence –

if they cried, we did not hear their pain,
seeing only their pips like glowing joints

in the malabowge of gazers on the sand,
each soul watching for a heavenly sign.

The meteors are profuse yet individual,
carrying wishes on their burning backs;

and if their agonies could be understood,
would they tell us who they died for?

Most things burn bright and brief,
and become the silence cinders leave,

when it talks of promises, praise, or prayers,

knowing none of these really matter,
except as a candle in the night.

Rain Delay

By night, the sound of neighbourhood hoses
chattered with artificial rain until dawn

silenced their coils and grass glistened.
With evening, every blade burnt blond,

I heard the rasp of lawn chair voices,
pitiless cries uttered from garages,

a beer in one hand, despair in the other,
and every vanity was contained in thirsts

no earthly mercies could ever slake,
the tears of broken angels no one dried.

What We Talk About When We Talk About Love

To love is to carry a lengthy catalog
of passions, always planting seedlings

wherever we go to populate the forests,
fields, green mountains, and oceans

resolute and calm after the soft hours,
of a night when dreaming is holding on,

signing our names on a weedy tideline
of great oceans with all the world offers,

the contract to which lovers agree,
the hand behind the covenant

of devotion, turning and the sun rising,
and the stars nest in your soft hands.

To think of love is to think of the world
and all that's in it, and if that is too much,

let us think of each other, our footsteps
on the autumn leaves beneath our feet

and round, full harvest moon rising above,
glowing, yellow, and clear enough to see by.

Curriculum

That was the spring they fell in love.
They fell in love over watered coffee
and were infatuated in Chaucer class.
They could turn a German tutorial to bliss.
Their blood boiled with falling love.

They fell in love and nothing caught them.
They fell with madness, their bodies screaming.
They flung their limbs around each other.
They fell but never hit the ground.

Falling was rapture. It belied their world.
The lucky grew wings the moment they fell.
Others thought falling would last forever.
They wrote their finals with fuddled minds.
They wrote poems on their finals that lived and died.

And what did it matter?
They learned so much more –
how headaches made the heart grow fonder,
how gut pain made each parting hell.
They learned to stare at the pages of books.
They learned to knot a tongue to a tongue.

The wind said come love with me and be my life.
The sky said come, come spread your wings.
This is your first lab in outright rejoicing.
The only science is the science you invent.

Love was the answer to the final question.
Turn over the examination paper.
It asked them to describe what they had learned,
and those who only studied for the test,
those whose lives were eaten in learning,
was it right to mark them pass or fail?

Love plus love was squared as the sum,
they learned the power of independent study,
the pedagogy of bodies footnoted in rapture:
they had to find the answers for themselves.
And when it didn't add up, they felt betrayed.
They felt their lives had been schooled in pain.

Such lovely stars had spread before them.
The curriculum was about astronomy now,
or the way the heavens dance around a life,
the intricate meanings of the pale spring stars.

Such delicate lights on a clear spring night
begged them to doodle in the margins of notes,
and each daisy or op art scrawl
wore points as sharp as a knife-thrower's kit,
with instructions on how to hit the heart.
They earn their degrees in degrees of pain.

Birds Look at the World as if They Didn't Fly

Because they never look at me directly
they remind me of someone in love,
the drive that sends a sparrow at a window,

the intensity that lives by guesswork
and opens its wing and never ceases
to leave me startled, passionate souls

with their ability to see what isn't there.
Isn't this the secret behind all devotion:
the power to perceive the imperceptible,

the gift that knows it is more than a gift,
the painful self-assurance that love
and birds serve the same purpose?

They rise. They fly. They know the air
is waiting for them to learn how the world
devours itself yet refuses to be held down.

And both sit in the palm of the hand
when they are being fed seeds
because love asks for nothing more –

the kernels of what is yet to come,
full of grace and gracefulness, the world
that is waiting to grow beyond itself.

Come live with me and greet the dawn.
Be my sunrise as I nest within your arms.
Teach me the blue of a clear and cloudless sky.

Shadows

I must remember to put away my shadows
when I am finished playing with them –

must pick up the flat one on the broadloom
and roll it up for the next time I lie down;

must peel the dark clown off the walls
because it won't stop playing the fool;

and the shadow of the past that wants
to jump out and scream there's more to come.

The shadow of my hands and face, especially
my nose catches changes in the air

and the scent of dinner cooking or the dog
wet after being out in the rain or flowers blooming

in the garden – these things are real because
they are shadows and they never go away,

and their darkness is simply a disguise
because they are my shadows and I am filled

with light, even when I am sleeping
and my eyes are open wide to see my dreams.

Reading Poetry to an Old Man

The only person present
is an old man who snores.
The three organizers leave,
asking from the door –

cream, one sugar, or two?
Even old men need to dream.
In Ernest Hemingway's story
about a widower and his brandy,

the waiters debate the question
of why he goes on living.
This is a clean, well-lit
bookstore and I have travelled

more than five hours to be here,
and the owners
insist I have to read.
Old man, shadow of my future,

do not open your eyes.
Let me sing to you of the sea,
her lithe body in green waves,
glistening as she approaches,

and how you think of her
as the words you couldn't find
or starlight that eluded you
before she broke the spell.

Acknowledgements

Some of the poems in this collection have appeared previously:

"Friendship is a Summer that Never Sheds Its Leaves" appeared in *Vallum*.

"Mount Everest" and "Apiary" appeared in the chapbook, *Telling the Bees* published by the magazine/press, Libretto, in Lagos, Nigeria.

"The Work" won the Guernsey Poetry Prize and appeared on buses and terminal advertisements in the Channels Islands.

"Symbols" appeared in the *Windsor Review* published by the University of Windsor.

"The Beautiful Neanderthals" appeared in *Lummox*.

"Rising Water" appeared in *Queen's Quarterly*.

"On First Looking into Bark's Rumi" was runner-up for the *Freefall Poetry Prize* and was published by *Freefall*.

"Jasmine Tea" and "The Best Time to Grow a Beard" appeared in *The Beauty of Being Elsewhere* edited by John B. Lee and published by Hidden Brook Press.

The author wishes to express his heartfelt thanks to the editors and publishers of those magazines and anthologies that featured his work with a special vote of gratitude to the following individuals for their kindness and support: Marty Gervais, John B. Lee, James Deahl, James Carson. Thank you for your keen editorial eye, Bruce Hunter. A special vote of gratitude to my publisher Michael Mirolla for this continued kindness and support, and thank you to Margaret Meyer, Dr. Carolyn Meyer, Katie Meyer, and my wife, Kerry Johnston.

About the Author

Bruce Meyer is the author of more than 70 books of poetry, short stories, flash fiction, and non-fiction. His most recent books of poems are *McLuhan's Canary* (Guernica Editions) and *Grace of Falling Stars* (Black Moss Press). His most recent works of fiction are *Magnetic Dogs* (Guernica Editions) and *Flashes in the Dark: Sweet Things* (Mosaic Press). A keen writer and promoter of flash fiction (very short stories), he co-edited *This Will Only Take a Minute: Canadian Flash Fiction* (Guernica Editions) with Michael Mirolla. He lives in Barrie, Ontario, and teaches at Georgian College. A recent recipient of a liver transplant, Meyer urges everyone to sign the donor portion of their driver's license.

Printed by Gauvin Press
Gatineau, Québec